BEAVERS

Curious Kids Press

Beavers

The beaver is in the rodent family. In fact, it is the second largest (the largest is the capybara). This animal is best known for building dams. The North American beaver's numbers once reached around 60 million, but now has been reduced to about 6 million. This is due to extensive hunting of this animal for its pelt. The beaver is an industrious animal and really cool. Let's explore the world of this rodent to see what else we can discover. Read on..

Where in the World?

Did you know there are beavers in Europe? The Eurasian beaver is found in Europe. The North American beaver can be found in Canada, throughout the United States and into parts of northern Mexico. It will always live by a water source, like rivers or wetlands, where it can build its dam and be safe from predators.

The Body of a Beaver

Did you know the beaver has a stocky body? Beavers continue to grow throughout their lifetime. Males can reach weights of around 55 pounds. Females will be smaller. Their legs are shorter with webbed back feet. Their front paws have 5 toes on each paw. Each toe has a sharp claw on the end of it.

The Beaver's Tail

Did you know the tail of a beaver is really flat? This rodent has a large flat tail that is shaped like a paddle for a boat. The beaver's tail helps steer this animal when it is moving logs to its dam. Its tail is also black and scaley. When the beaver is on land, its broad tail helps it balance when it is carrying heavy loads.

The Beaver's Fur

Did you know the beaver's fur is very thick? It has 2 layers; long fur on top and short fine hairs underneath. The top coat keeps this animal waterproof, while the undercoat keeps the beaver warm. The beaver needs to groom to keep its coat waterproof. An oily substance called, castor, is produced by the beaver. It spreads the castor around its body by grooming.

The Beaver's Teeth

Did you know the beaver has 2 huge front teeth? This animal's front teeth stick out the front of its mouth. This is so the beaver can cut wood while underwater. The beaver's teeth are very sharp and can saw through small trees and branches. This animal's teeth never stop growing, so chewing on tough trees, helps keep them trim.

What a Beaver Eats

Did you know the beaver only eats the bark from wood, not the entire branch? Beavers only eat plants. This makes them, vegetarians. This animal likes to eat cattail shoots in the spring and summer months. In the autumn and winter seasons, the beaver will eat shrubs and tree bark.

The Beaver's Dam

Did you know the beaver's dam can be harmful to humans? A beaver's dam will change the natural flow of a river or a lake. This can sometimes create flooding for the area it is in. The beaver works all night to build a basic dam. It uses mud, stones and sticks it has collected.

The Beaver's Lodge

Did you know the beaver makes a home called, a lodge? Lodges can either be surrounded by water or on the banks of a shore. The lodge is made from sticks and mud. There are at least 2 water-filled tunnels leading in and out of the lodge. Beavers do not hibernate and will store sticks for food.

Inside the Beaver Lodge

Did you know the beaver's lodge is warm and dry inside? The beaver's home has a big chamber for eating, sleeping and to groom and raise their young. This mammal will collect soft materials like, grasses, reeds and wood chips for its bedding. It is changed often to keep its home neat and tidy.

The Beaver as Prey

Did you know the beaver has many predators? This rodent is hunted by a lot of predators, both big and small. Common predators of the beaver include the lynx, owls, wolverines, bears, coyotes, northern river otters, wolves and hawks. People also still hunt the beaver for its pelt and occasionally its meat.

Beaver Talk

Did you know the beaver uses its tail to make a loud "slapping" sound on the water? This is done when the beaver is alarmed. A beaver can hiss and snort when it is upset.or whine when it is in pain. Another sound is "churring." This is a sign of contentment. Soft mumbling noises may mean the beaver has a lot on his mind.

The Beaver Mom and Dad

Did you know beavers pair for life? Adult beavers will find one mate and stay with that one until one of them dies. Both the male and female beavers build the lodge. After mom has her babies, she will care for them, while dad defends the lodge and his family.

Baby Beavers

Did you know baby beavers are called, kits? Baby beavers are born in a litter of up to 6 kits. They are born in the lodge where they will nurse milk from their mother. Kits will remain with the parents until they are about 2 years-old. At this time they will leave to start their own family.

Life of a Beaver

Did you know beavers are very social? Beavers live in family units consisting of a mother, father, 2 year-old kits and newborn young. Sometimes beavers will build an addition onto their lodge when the family gets too big. If left alone to thrive, beavers can live to be around 24 years old.

Quiz

Question 1: What is the beaver known for?

Answer 1: Building dams and its flat tail

Question 2: What shape is the beaver's tail?

Answer 2: It is paddle-shaped

Question 3: What part of the beaver's body never stops growing?

Answer 3: Its two front teeth

Question 4: What is the beaver's home called?

Answer 4: A lodge

Question 5: How many kits can the mother beaver have?

Answer 5: Up to 6

Thank you for checking out another addition from Curious Kids Press! Make sure to check out Amazon.com for many other great titles.